MILLENNIAL PULP

A Progression through Poetry

Joone Alberto Tena

[Contents]

[Prologue]

I began writing this book in 2017 without the intent of it ever being a book. The election results that year left a wake of uncertainty in the minds of my immediate community. Friends, family, and neighbors began turning on one another. The airwaves were saturated with ongoing controversy. No media was safe from the specter of radicalized ideology. It felt like every day there was something new and the fear of missing out kept us glued to the mainstream. The constant flux was unbearable. The stimuli. The dread.

The following year only paid tribute to its predecessor and so forth. The constant rocking ship left the look of anguish on the faces of an already depleted civilization. All I could do was watch. With my journal in hand, I watched, as another massive wave took shape before our next step. Hence, the dawn of the virus and the year of isolation that followed. In an instant the noise was depleted as the entire world fell silent in a collective fear. Sadly, all I could do was watch.

This is my obligation...

This is Millennial Pulp

[Millennial Pulp]

At the end of the empire-
I await your jolly whistle
I await the ash to float atop the river-
Where it belongs
Where it goes to the lowest point
Where it goes to evaporate

At the end of the empire-
I swore to you it would be
Warned you
Cornered you with fang and foam
Till your eyes swelled with blood

I beg your last drop of mercy
In dialects I have yet to learn
In lands I have yet to travel
You lain your battered flag

I beg you take your rest
To lick your wounds
Perched in the high oak
Nude and always bright
Awaiting this unstoppable

[Panic Rooms]

Weeping tired
Soft slugs in hot sinking sand
Ruins and tombs for those who wish to stay
I won't. I can't. I didn't know any better
That this snowball could be a war
That this stone could be a wall
Leave me shaking in a pillow bag
By and down
To and fro
Onward and back to the square

[Minding Murky]

Knowing is only half
Being is a chore
Walking sores
Heavy cleats
Feeling of falling north

Our porcelain story
Heavy bottom
Boring
Brimmed with pennies
Lint and squabble

Prone to reach
The olive brush
In time for doves
Before the flood

Here and now
There from here
All about
This pendulum

Screams of terror
A pinch of hair
My broken nails
Have yet to fail

However long
What's come of this

I've found a home
In murky bliss

[The Brux]

Paranoia
Don't know why
Paranoia
Don't know why
Release
Unclench
Un-Be for a while
Make it stop!

Unplug
Untouch
Undo your hair
Make it stop!

Unwatch
Untame
Unwind
Make it stop!
Paranoia
Don't know why
Paranoia
Don't know why

[Bristles]

Hands down soldier
Tonight, sleep well
Tonight, no chills
No remembering...
Those sirens
Only silence
Only your breath slowing
And the bristles in wind

Hands down
Hands down

You can do no more
Only love...
To forget
And snicker a bit
Take your time soldier
Tire slowly
You are rare
But not yet gone
Free and somehow lost
No more
No more left to do
But smile
Rest easy soldier
Peace is nigh
The everlasting afoot

[Laugh!]

When your friend falls
Same as your enemy
Give it time
That's all
Often funny
Is the outcome
Don't fret
Lament or die
It's too funny when you do
When your friends fall
As do your enemies
Give it time
Grin and weep
All is woe
Choose
Smile or death
It's too funny when you do

[Standby]

Itch for it
For it is far
And you are young

Tire me with nudity
Till I wish no more

Be that it may
You continue to wait

Watching and believing
For something by evening

Morning arises
With little surprises

[Blinking]

Does it make for perfect conversation
To know we have yet to be alone?
In the wild with open oyster
Eyes as bright as the sundog spots
Too in love to unclench
To unravel, how it just dissolves
Natural
In pictures only in our heads
The quiet films that awaken us
To an everlasting ease
Became a wave sliced by torrents
By pirates. Or unending voices from sirens
We had chased; till we found ourselves here
Woven loose between my lungs
Squeezing every bit of you
While dunking my eyes in a cosmic tar
And somehow expecting your return by dawn
The moments to be had
The blinks that await the seconds
Keeping time as usual
And we go with them, nowhere
Only to what is next
Where our sail has yet to take air
If there ever was a single direction
And how to call it by name
Where we have yet to be
Blinking without question

[Graveyard Shift]

I dream of hotels beyond the clouds
Drawing the silk curtains and privatizing a bath
In a jungle. In this city once again.
Lobbies filled with blurry, drunk faces
Rubbish; hand in hand with its shade
Spawning conversation with the strange
Their empty philosophies becoming evident
Waving false flags and handing out pamphlets
-like soap box junkies

I ask for directions
Where the apples grow to die
With a deck of cards and a forked tongue
I bore this fortune
Tricking the whores and winos
Calling the rot: 'cider'
Pawning fowl
Trading secrets
Dancing barefoot
Trampling the marble floors
Under an uncut chandelier

[Ode to Lemon]

Shaking you in my copper mug
Sample this...
Numbness
A disposition worth understanding
A morning worthy of waking to
Glory in stillness
Holy with fault
I'll recede till its death
In hopes we bloom

Swollen with youth
I fell for you
Tardy
As always
Weary
On arrival
You locked your fingers in mine
Birthing the orchids
Sharing breath in serene color
Until the shape of white took you away

[Slow Races]

I always have to be somewhere for some reason
I am never late though
I always knew how to win
I just never tried
I always knew it matter more to you
I was only there to watch
I forgot why I'm here
I just know it's not for me

[Tender Crimes]

I forgave you
For nothing
For your posture in nature
I suppose you are guilty
For the power you have
For the gifts you have been given
Smite me for my love of beauty if need be
It has filled my chalice allowing for nothing more
As if harmony were nigh; in that truth can live
To persevere without a king or a nag to call:
'friend'

I forgave you
For nothing
For a day to be you
Numb in thought and heavy with prayer
Chanting mantras like a hooligan
Climbing the mountains without camp
No worry. No sadness.
No fear of the worlds below
I forgave you
For nothing
For nothing needs forgiving

[Everybody Wins]

You want to be special
You want it to mean something
You aren't wrong
They can't be wrong

We followed them into war; into fashion
Befriended the loners and conversed with the
strange
At least till nothing more could be said

As silence paves the way from here
Silence as it all falls down
You blamed your neighbor
Your comrades
Left in pools of plastic blood
Floating like islands
Chests bloated with the sea
Mouthful of precious stones

You watched as if you were special
Need not your interference
As it all continues to be
As someone to look and someone to know

How it feels. How it felt when it was over
A winter without wind
A summer smothered in cloud
How special you were
What a tragedy it is

[Chew]

The noise is beyond bright
Becoming racket
Those clanking spoons
During their perverted talk
The news
The distractions
Our certainty is not without dread
As mourning is paired with pride

If only a mild day
In the gullets of eels
If only a second without sound
To grasp the truth of the light
I would trade my voice
To chew
Swallow
Choke
On faith
For what is left
Births what will be
Somehow, a meaningless awareness
One I often doubt
And one that more often follows

[En Route]

I'm raptured by the focal points
Spearing outward in rings of gravity
Holding me close to you
Allowing me nowhere
Allocating an inch of breath

Dense with silk and silver
Chasing opposite your footprints
Into danger on the riverbeds
Squeezing my knuckles like a bear trap
Turning me
Changing me
Losing me now
As I pull free

Liberating from sorrow
No longer lamenting my belongings
Soaring inches from the faces of cliffs
Nowhere to go
No one I have be
No one waiting with the lights on

Only this absolute
Bearing the absurd

[The East Mountain]

Allow me in your foam
A squeeze of embrace if you will
As the morning star makes you visible
You dance before my gaze
My love
I'm lost in you
Like seeds in a wine cask
You carried me to my next step
Awaiting my recompose with patience
Forming diamonds at the crests of your cheeks
If only I were as resilient
Instead, this bone turns to feast
Then to rock and back to nothing
If only to use my time as you
To shadow your stillness
As one with your ghost
My love
I'm lost in you
If infinity ever were
In those burning seconds
To be awake
Knowing it was only a dream
My reflection or a chance to be
I would dwell toward eternal comfort
In helpless flow with little mind

[City Life]

Bank the sidewalks with crimson
Up to the neck
In waves of collapse
Outlined in yellow chalk

In forgetting gravitas
When laying brick made of dung
We have failed to read from palm
Losing our tongues in the fire
Breeding vice in a dance

Handing the keys to kings
As they idle on velvet rugs
Overlooking a wasted village
Hungry for salvation
High on cornish liquids and floral dew
Circling the mongrels as prey
Dizzy as a bee
Angry as a punctured bull
As deaf as the morning bell

[The Cathartic]

What better day to have:

A broken watch
A good friend
An endless bottle like the barrel itself
A pine fire and some string to pluck

[Blue Dress]

Our humble room
Deep in conversation
What is next?
Either I clean my soul
Or I live without you
I want to be a better man
With a knowing that keeps you safe
Although it just seems like waiting
Curling your body into mine
Feeling your eyes have already wandered
Beyond our humble room
Into the admiration of the exterior
Into the mind of another

The pictures have changed
The windows allow air
And you're wearing a dress I've never seen before
Firmly content, in a full bloom
Golden from the sun's kisses
Clutched by my wretched hunger
Nearly to certain deprivation
Instead of letting free be free
I awaited a barren response
An ultimatum or a possible outing

Our humble room
Dear bird, it has become your cage
This place, I know it
You're too beautiful to stay

Better barefoot at the party
Evading my notice
Birthing a love in silence
As cladding welds behind you
Leaving a once bright room
Wearing a dress, I've never seen before

[The Fuse]

Elongated vulgarity
Our era of illusion has bred us this way
Dining on the behalf of the young
Leaving a trail of crumbs across the forest beds
Leading to a paradise without coordinates
That sweet, promised land
Long after the fuse has burned

Wiping clean the remnants of our perversion
Off the tile in a spume collective
Emptying the towers by erasing the numbers
In a purity that stings with sanitation
Diving headfirst

Void of the illusion that once was
Economy and country
Like a boulder at the crest
Tipping on the bones of those that rolled it there
In winds without reserve
All whilst the desperate wild looks on
Cracking the concrete with feral vine
Piercing the night with an opal glow
Trading their lives for salvation
Long after the fuse has burned

[Unpacking]

Unnaturally...
Born with kindness
Seeking warmth in armor
Or the approval of others
A high-pitched chant
In subliminal acceptance
Of your skin
And how your hips make like hills

Under my tentacle sensory
Lighting every cell with a sodium burn
As your laughter extends to my next life
In dreams of your dance
Gazing helplessly like a salivating dog

In the depths of shady brothels
Under laws beyond thought
Cradling with care
An old song or a piece of cloth
Something with a scent
Or a meaning my claws have yet met

To pull you
Draped in your spare seconds
Feeling more between my fingers
Then in my palms
I lack a squeeze
In the pinch of your watch
Drowned by your perfume in the pillow bags

Waking to a pale presence
Stamped between your eyes
As a means of end; with plenty of notice
This nitrate ready to release in pokes
This blue fire without a name
Only visiting during the ache
Calming my gut only after I've drank the sea

In a dreamy filter
Aboard your coat tail
Awaiting the incoming in absolute cheer
Becoming a porridge for you
As passive reads or a wallflower begging to be
picked

[Bland]

This will pass
This will pass
To whomever you are
Nothing stays past a couple of days
Unless we want it to
We petty boar for wanting more
Cheery as can be
Best to know of letting go
If there's any hope for me

This will pass
This will pass

Allowing for anew
Telling all the strangers
All our neighbors in pursuit
This will pass
This will pass
Buying a round of pints
Wishing all in wellness
As we pass away the night

[Capital]

The sun continues
The day as we know
A pacing for profit
Seeking luxury
In crowded buses making loops
This all for nothing
Crippling nowhere
Nor asking direction

Whilst ghost abandon the cog
Leaving the machine unmanned
Tamed only by itself
Chewing away at forbidden fruit
In cemeteries close to home

The moon continues
The night as we know
Primordial in its swallow
Pumping sulfur into the atmosphere
Playing on a chip tabletop
Up and down the neon grid
Keeping this box awake
In a feverish insomnia
Aimlessly nomadic in the finest attire

[Nurse]

Always in your romantic dialect
Even in mumbles I catch wind of rose
As you were
A jade statue bouncing light and noise like toys
As a symbol of tempered justice
In all your stoicism
Void of worrying in a harp cocoon
Letting all be what it is
This forfeit in my hold
Until you conspire your escape
Cradling a lasting image of me
In a muscle cauldron
Tucked in the silt like a layer of skin
In knowing no surprise at my return
Carrying vanity like a wet newspaper
This fragile
Even at a passing glance
In all hopes for a cent of composure
To conjure a floating ark
Sparing me your tide
Carving me of stone
Calling me by name
From a spiral pull
This enigma
With no bouts of end
Compressing space between us
Dropping me at your door
In a wolf-like cosmetic
With symptoms of bliss

Delirium and bullet wounds
Pleading a frail understanding
As you nurse what is left
An array of shocked sensory
Whispering bottomless love
Giving as the saline juice
In an unsaid chill
Madly itching for a cure

[Order]

Together in a sweat
With a gate to pass
One that is proof of flesh
With tales of abrasion
These forever marks
Contemplating a height above the chapels
As your human oath
I bore every moment in your eye
As a sea sponge
Recording your laugh
In my naked allowance
On a chrome platter
Only by your favor
As a dunce
As a sheep out of count
Demanding the wildest admiration
Diving out of your dream
In a sequence that demands focus
Within you
Shaped as a horn
In waves of holy smoke
Sounding the creator
With a clanking tongue
Made of an erratic mantra
Repeating tales of a boring day
In a lexicon soon to be spoken
As a film outside your teeth
Without a fool to blame
This pointing out

This name calling
Of endless knowing
And forever presence
In perfect order

[The Seed]

Unlike any retrieve
In colors off the grid
Breaking the simulacra
With a knowing of numbers
Sadly, pilled to see
All there was in a valley view
Respirating a song of liberation
In a tone, best for insects
With eyes only for the abstract
Thus, scaling ladders that break the clouds
While crossing bridges that part the sea
All in all, was hand in hand
Locked in a twisted pillar
Comforted by stillness in absolution
Up...
Until the clay earth breaks free

[The Fetus]

Wandered here
In a breath of azure figure
This macabre geometry emanating from its
center
Jointed by wadded angles in a boiled spin
Filled with blood and awareness
Ruled by a communal stupor
Begging a pestering curiosity
For nearness
To feel the vine
To surveil the endless terrain
Within a wall of entrails
Bearing all that has yet to be
As a freckle in the sun's wake
By some circumference of warmth
Resembling a tired story
Of a game within itself
Warranting a stalemate with a calming ecstasy
With chariots of primordial fruit
Thought
Becoming bone
Identity and language
In a spiral of placement
Rooting where it falls
As feathers from a flustered crow
Soon a marble slate
Demanding to be named

[Unwanted Guests]

Instantly falling in line
Flat footed on spherical stone
Oh, frequent spins!
Tosses with bouts of expansion
How the center pushes all away from you
As keeping close could cause this somehow
As mimicked in romance novels
Stories of our truth with unending crime
Breaking young hearts with intolerable nearness
Giving unearthed secrets the appearance of coal
Evolving into parasites
Or something of silhouettes in nightmares
Substances that took love only as an ingredient
Baking a sinister presence in every family home
As I had always known:
That what is good for the world is not good for
your family
What is good for your family is never good for
the world
If choosing should lead you here
I assure you...
You can't be wrong
Regardless of what they say
If bouts of uncharacterized behavior carries you
So be it
You can't be wrong
If there ever was such a maddening thing
To see in a rotunda mirror-scape
All the angles awaiting your judgement

It's knowing acceptance; that births a soon to
be had freedom
It is only the twisted informant acting in
duality
Telling fragrant lies of ongoing opposition
If only, what was yours could soon be mine
Making jest toward pestering reptiles
To manipulate the believers so they see for
themselves
A lake of fire capable of burning the past
Led by a river with no remorse for itself

[No More Than What Is]

I don't want to try for a new love anymore
I am tired, you see!
Tired of looking into the eyes of my hospice
Praying for a mold that lasts this life
Instead bearing in hand, the ashes of my
shortcomings
A promise to you
A knowing I was only half the man
A departure with no mercy
Boiling hope to a flaccid muscle

This ignorance has brought me little bliss
As this imagination wanders without master
Continuing to bring me here
In airwaves by your magnificent shape
Repetitively swerving way in my attempted
existence
For as badly as I want to blame you; I love you!
I've learned it hasn't changed
It is unforgiving and endless in its shame
For you have found a forward star worthy of your
descent

Go then! If so!

I'm only burdened by a simple wishing
One of which that expands my plate
To continue beyond the summit
Without your voice leading me to scold

I don't want to try for a new love anymore
The journey to know one isn't worth the walk
Your heft leaves print along my spine
How can I?
Carry another?
Without rings of you
Tangling my every step
I'd wish it no other way
To remember the brightness
As it was
Without word of anew
Heckled by a never arriving dawn
Funneled in your nocturnal breathe
Keeping me caged
Taming me to no more than what is

[Duo]

I doubt there could be anything left to spare
You see, I was lost in the innocence of lilies
Picking and therefore killing
In their finest moments and when least expected
Only man and a God could of course...
Carry on afterward

Clear the mind - Sweet one!
Bear your cluster of breath in bushes of savage
foliage
Tolerant to the abuse of this desert abysmal
Coveted by swarms of waxy thorns
Repelling any potential patron

In brush canals, home to the whiskered species
Viper fish!
Torrents of turtles with teeth
Snapping your line nearing to your collar ribbon
Grasping every wish to protect your own pulse
And even then
You've done so...
A whole beginning to end
With no recollection

But I see you!
If no one else does
Working in silent reflection
Revealing a bait for fools
Heavy with crude fats and wooden fillers

Benevolent to the swine and all its vice
Disappointing as it is:
Expecting such ascension from curious pawns
Tongue-tied and worthy of a whip

Scarring stories
Supple in gore
These broken down minutes
In grids to colorless blocks
Now a pearl
Bright with a piercing arrival

Oh, purveyor of the swirling rods
Burning around the collective duo
Oblique.
Odd.
Ongoing.
We're finally together
At last!

About the Author

Joone Alberto Tena was born and raised in Albuquerque, New Mexico. Drawn to writing at an early age as a means of coping with childhood troubles, Joone eventually decided to go public with many of his privatized works. Beginning as an act of avid journaling, eventually evolved into a prolific desire to share ideas of revolution, existentialism, spirituality, and self-care in the abstract medium of poetry.

www.ingramcontent.com/pod-product-compliance
Lightning Source LLC
LaVergne TN
LVHW051428080426
835508LV00022B/3290